D1294417

Going for a walk with a line

a step into the world of modern art

By Douglas and Elizabeth MacAgy

DOUBLEDAY & COMPANY, INC. GARDEN CITY, NEW YORK

4446

This one is for Ian

Library of Congress Catalog Card Number
59–5899. Copyright © 1959 by Douglas MacAgy
and Elizabeth MacAgy. All Rights Reserved.
Printed in the United States of America.

Foreword

This is a book that says when you are young the shortest distance between two points is not a straight line because there are too many sidelines to discover. A straight line to anywhere would be a bore that got you wherever you were going without any of the thousand adventures any child knows are to be had on the way anywhere.

The only hurry of youth is that while there is all the time in the world to enjoy being alive, you'd better hurry up and enjoy it—every inch of the way.

Once grown up, we are likely to enjoy less because we are overwhelmed by the fact that there isn't enough time to get everything done that there is to do, or that has to be done. For us this is where the artist comes in—to create pleasure in leisure for people of all ages. Artists remember, for themselves and for all of us—forever—everything imaginable from the greatest experience to the smallest.

The artist's line is in this way a line of youth that leads us from the world well known to worlds we no longer dream about or have time to think about, and sometimes into worlds we've never known.

Today most of us are apt to ground-hog it when we see our own shadow. We crawl back as if into a dark hole where we aren't forced to see ourselves or the day we live in. But surer than the sun, the artists can stir us out of ourselves. Through their eyes we may discover that looking at ourselves is not so bad after all. Often, when we're persuaded there's nothing but gloom all around us, the artists, looking at the same things we thought dull, find laughter; and the people we had supposed dormant, they find awake.

This unique and engaging presentation is as refreshing and varied as the works of art which form it. It excites the mind and wins the eye as the pictures take on their own life. The book's charm will escape neither artist nor child, and others, I believe, will find it revealing.

VINCENT PRICE

PÈRE JUNIET'S CART by Henri Rousseau.
1908. Oil, 38½ x 51½ inches.* Courtesy Rousseau
Exhibition at the Sidney Janis Gallery, 1951.

*Height precedes width.

Once, on bright days
when little white clouds
looked like twirly mustaches up
near the edge of the sky,
a nice dappled horse
used to take his family
and his friends
all dressed up
for a walk
to see the sights.

And sometimes, all dressed up, it was fun to stroll, stopping

to look this way and that, or else

PLACE DE LA CONCORDE by Edgar Degas.
1875. Oil, 31⅛ x 46½ inches. Copyright by
S. P. A. D. E. M., Paris.

to scamper straight ahead like a proud little puppy.

LEASH IN MOTION by Giacomo Balla. 1912.
Oil, 35¾ x 43⅜ inches. Collection A. Conger
Goodyear, New York.

Sometimes, too, it is fun to imagine stepping up

From OVER VITEBSK by Marc Chagall. *A detail.*

right into the sky, or better still, really to

OVER VITEBSK by Marc Chagall. 1920 (after
a painting of 1914). Oil, 26⅜ x 36½ inches. The
Museum of Modern Art, New York; acquired
through the Lillie P. Bliss Bequest.

run with a hoop through

From THE MYSTERY AND MELANCHOLY
OF A STREET by Giorgio de Chirico. 1914. Oil,
34¼ x 28⅛ inches. *A detail; the complete picture
is next.*

an almost empty street. Often, without knowing, grown-up people in cities

walk any which way and play hide-and-seek with great big buildings. At other

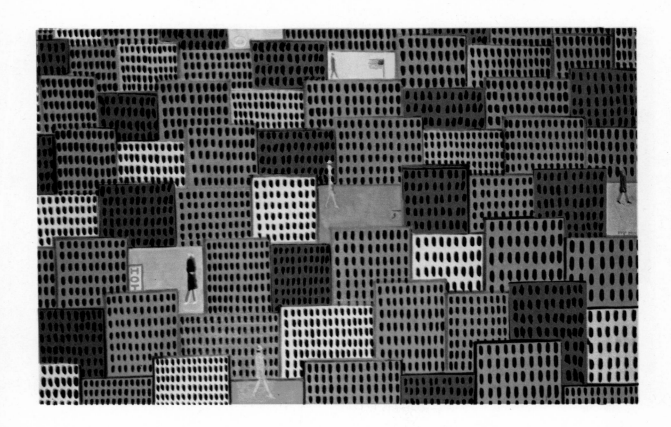

AMERICAN CITY by Evsa Model. 1943. Oil,
42 x 66 inches. Collection Rudi Blesh, New York.

times they march happily together, holding big bright flags .... But.

FLAG DAY by William Doriani. 1935. Oil, 12¼
x 38¼ inches. Collection Sidney Janis, New York.

ARTISTS may sit still and draw pictures of stepping out — even pictures of

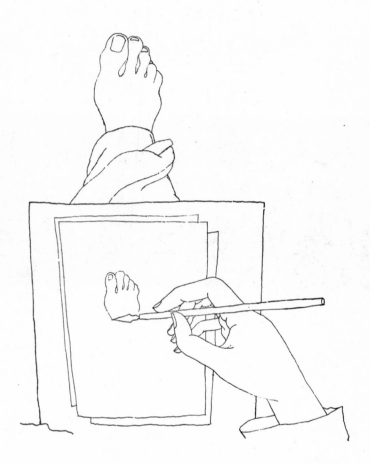

ART by Jean Cocteau. 1923. Pen and ink, 11 x 9
inches as originally reproduced. From "Dessins"
by Jean Cocteau, Librairie Stock, Delamain et
Boutelleau, Paris.

sprawly beetles on parade, leaving curvy bug trails. An artist may sit still

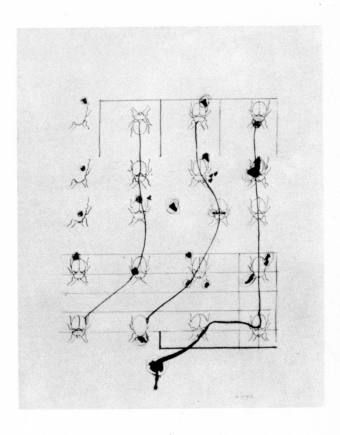

BEETLES by J. T. Baargeld. 1920. Pen and ink,
11½ x 9⅛ inches. The Museum of Modern Art,
New York; Purchase Fund.

with a pencil or brush and go for a "walk" with a line — up,

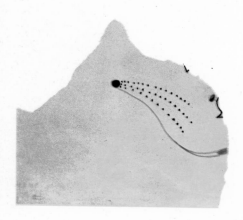

From THE HERMITAGE by Joan Miro. *A detail.*

up, up to a tiny castle and a tree like a flame

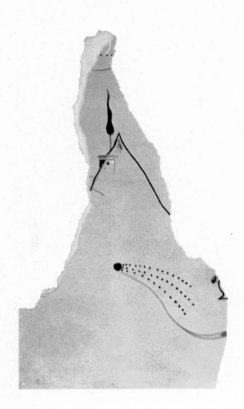

From THE HERMITAGE by Joan Miro. *A detail.*

high on a zigzag hill that touches the starry, moony, sunny sky.

THE HERMITAGE by Joan Miro. 1924. Oil, 45 x
57½ inches. Philadelphia Museum of Art; Louise
and Walter Arensberg Collection.

Or his picture may "dance" in very straight lines

From BROADWAY BOOGIE WOOGIE by Piet
Mondrian. *A detail.*

and turn sharp corners up, and down, and across —

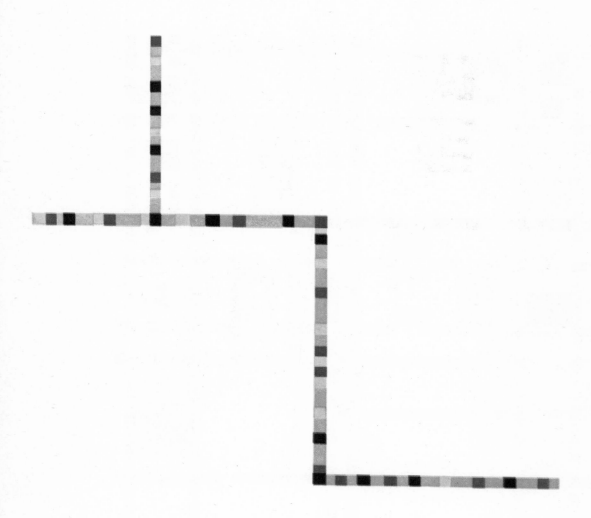

From BROADWAY BOOGIE WOOGIE by Piet
Mondrian. 1942–43. Oil, 50 x 50 inches. The
Museum of Modern Art, New York. *A detail;
the complete picture is next.*

jumping, skipping along to the edge as

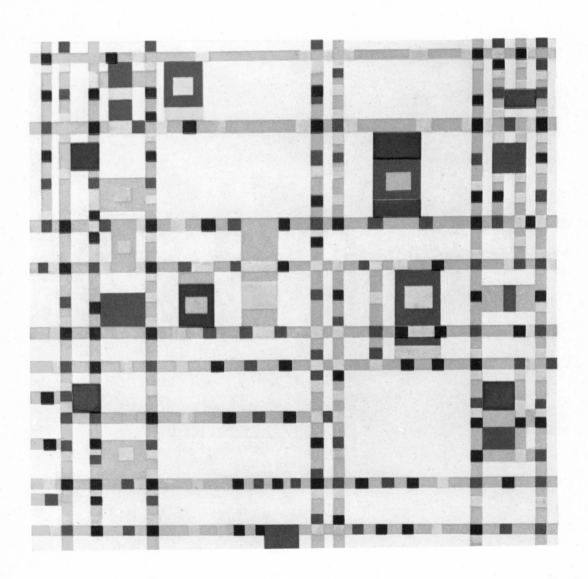

chalk lines of hopscotch mark out a jig.

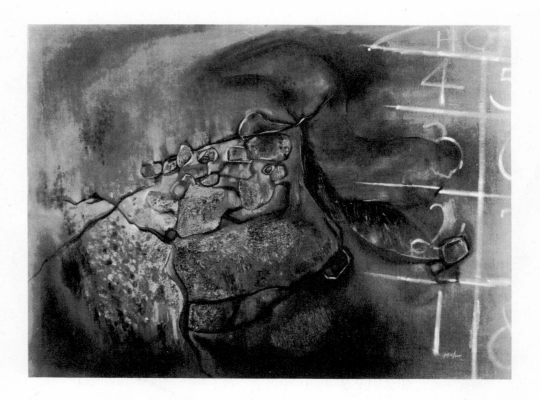

HOPSCOTCH by Loren MacIver. 1940. Oil, 27 x 35⅞ inches. The Museum of Modern Art, New York; Purchase Fund.

Everybody knows that pictures do not paint themselves. In the twinkling of

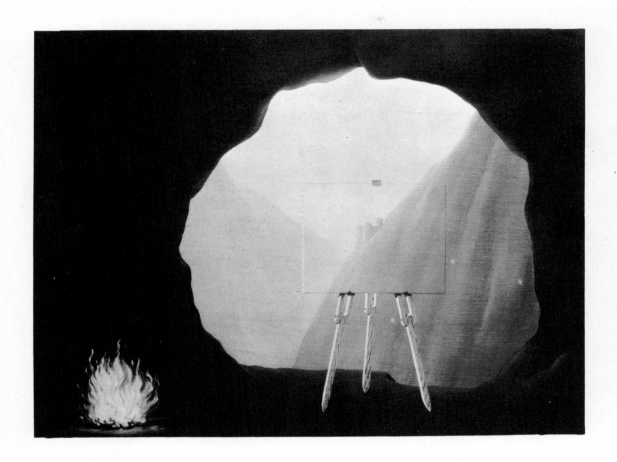

THE HUMAN CONDITION by René Magritte.
1935. Oil, 21½ x 28¾ inches. Collection Basil
Wright, London.

an artists's eye, a picture may half-pretend it is a peek at the sky. Or a

THE FALSE MIRROR by René Magritte. 1928.
Oil, 21¼ x 37⅞ inches. The Museum of Modern
Art, New York; Purchase Fund.

picture might show what he sees in his mind, and not what he looks at outside.

THE ARTIST LOOKS AT NATURE by Charles
Sheeler. 1943. Oil, 21 x 18 inches. The Art Insti-
tute of Chicago. Photo: courtesy TIME; copyright
1955, Time Inc.

Sometimes lines walk along paths without a look at a thing. They

PAINTER WITH A MODEL KNITTING by
Pablo Picasso. 1927. Etching, 7⅝ x 11⅜ inches.
Illustration for "Le Chef-d'Oeuvre Inconnu" by
Balzac, 1931. The Museum of Modern Art, New
York; gift of Henry Church.

circle and slant like rainy-day

**LINE CONSTRUCTION by Alexander Rod-
chenko. 1920. Colored inks, 12¾ x 7¾ inches.
The Museum of Modern Art, New York.**

games with wonderful names — Backgammon, Dominoes,

AMERICANA by Charles Sheeler. 1931. Oil, 48
x 36 inches. Collection Mr. and Mrs. Milton Low-
enthal, New York.

Checkers and Chess — when you

THE CHESSBOARD by Juan Gris. 1917. Oil,
28¾ x 39⅜ inches. The Museum of Modern Art,
New York; Purchase Fund.

sit very still, and still you will move

GAME OF CHESS by Jacques Villon. 1904.
Drypoint, 11¹³⁄₁₆ x 15⁹⁄₁₆ inches. The Museum of
Modern Art, New York; Purchase Fund.

neat blocks and balls on a squarely ruled board, or

CHESS SET designed by Josef Hartwig. 1924.
Wood, natural and stained black. Manufactured
by the Bauhaus, Weimar. The Museum of Modern
Art, New York.

fit tidy toy houses to a crisscross of streets.

MENTAL CALCULUS by René Magritte. 1931.
Oil, 26 x 45¾ inches. Collection Mrs. James
Laughlin, Norfolk, Connecticut.

Like toys on a floor, pictures are things that play make-believe games —

TOYS OF A PRINCE by Giorgio de Chirico.
1914—15. Oil, 24 x 19¾ inches. The Museum of
Modern Art, New York; Purchase Fund.

where people sit like shadows near trees and a house, and become, turned

PARANOIC FACE by Salvador Dali. 1935. Oil,
7½ x 9 inches. Collection Edward F. W. James,
Sussex, England.

on end, the face of a giant half sunk in the sand — where

PARANOIC FACE by Salvador Dali.

the artist dreams of a long-ago land, and a river with

CLEOPATRA'S BARGE by André Bauchant. 1939.
Oil, 32 x 39⅜ inches. The Museum of Modern
Art, New York; Mrs. John D. Rockefeller, Jr.
Purchase Fund.

upside-down people — or where you may hunt

From CLEOPATRA'S BARGE by André Bauchant. *A detail of the foregoing picture.*

for a whisker-made elephant and other odd things

From DARK JUNGLE by Ynez Johnston. *A*
detail.

in a tangle of lines like a jungle.

DARK JUNGLE by Ynez Johnston. 1950. Casein
gouache, 23⅜ x 17⅞ inches. The Museum of
Modern Art, New York; Katharine Cornell Fund.

Lines may make moonlight that shines on a bird, or skitter

BIRD SINGING IN THE MOONLIGHT by
Morris Graves. 1938–39. Gouache, 26¾ x 30⅛
inches. The Museum of Modern Art, New York;
Purchase Fund.

and bounce like bugs flying among flowers.

INSECTS AT TWILIGHT by Charles Burch-
field. 1917. Watercolor, 14 x 19¾ inches. The
Museum of Modern Art, New York; gift of Mrs.
John D. Rockefeller, Jr.

One line may be twisted to shape a fat pig, and two may be pointed to make a

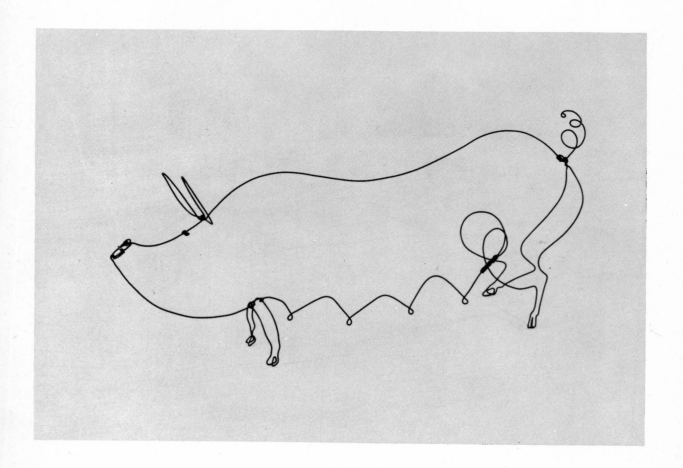

SOW by Alexander Calder. 1928. Wire construction, 17 inches long. The Museum of Modern Art,
New York; gift of the artist.

mustache which tells puzzle-world time on the face of a clock that watches.

THE EXACT HOUR by Wolfgang Paalen.
1935(?) Construction in wood. Photograph courtesy Marc Vaux, Paris.

Outlines are games to take you anywhere — even towards the moon, or else

DOG BARKING AT THE MOON by Joan
Miro. 1926. Oil, 28¾ x 36¼ inches. Philadelphia
Museum of Art; A. E. Gallatin Collection.

to look at thirsty puppy dogs, and empty glasses on a table.

STILL LIFE WITH THREE PUPPIES by Paul
Gauguin. 1888. Oil, 36⅛ x 24⅝ inches. The
Museum of Modern Art, New York; Mrs. Simon
Guggenheim Fund.

A line may dance, or it may walk, and you

DANCE by Jacques Villon. 1932. Oil, 15⅛ x 21⅝
inches. The Museum of Modern Art, New York;
gift of Mrs. Arthur L. Strasser.

may walk or slide or teeter with it.

TIGHTROPE WALKER by Paul Klee. 1923.
Color lithograph, 17½ x 10½ inches. The Museum
of Modern Art, New York.